LA FLORIDA

Bar Restaurant

Obispo & Monserrate Sts. Tels. M-5031 A-0004
Habana, Cuba

The Cradle of the Daiquiri Cocktail

*Where cocktails are a revelation
and food is most delicious : :*

Constantino Ribalaigna

SMALL - DINGER

½ Gordon Gin.	½ Ginebra Gordon.
½ Ron Baçardi.	½ Rhum Bacardi.
¼ Granadine.	¼ Granadine.
¼ Jugo Limón.	¼ Lemon Juice.
Hielo Frappé abundante. Bátese ligeramente y cuélese.	Frappé Ice. Shake and strain.

INTRODUCTION

Welcome to "Bar La Florida Cocktails 1935 Reprint".

La Florida, also known as the "Floridita," invented the Daiquiri. And even if they didn't as some may claim that in fact it was American mining engineers drinking at the Venus bar in Santiago that invented it, La Florida made it famous, with a little help from Papa.

Ernest "Papa" Hemingway, would meet friends like Spencer Tracy or Gary Cooper, and order a round of his drink, the "Papa Doble," a double Daiquiri mixture over a single serving of shaved ice.

This book was also the start of many misprints. The Daiquiri recipe calls for a Lemon Verde, translated literally means a "green lemon" which back then was a badly translated lime.

And when they ask for maraschino, it is maraschino liqueur they want, which is not a splash of neon red goop from the cherry jar no matter what the clerk wants to sell you.

Featuring many cocktails with measurements, it also covers more obscure drinks like absinthe drop, mojito, zazerac, Mary Pickford, Peggy Niles, and pisco punch.

This book is a time capsule of drinks at the time, which allows us to date the progression of drink popularity.

Cheers!

ACE más de cien años—en los sencillos tiempos de 1819—un bodegón típico se alzaba cabe de viejas murallas de la Puerta de Monserrate. Era una casona de ventanales buidos, adonde acudían petimetres, músicos, militares, síndicos, faranduleros, milicianos y hombres de toda laya, siempre gente bien, gustosos de saborear la sabrosa ginebra compuesta o el aguardiente de guindas...En sus quitrines, las damas bajo el quitasol de seda, sorbían, mientras eran cortejadas por sus galanes, sendos vasos de los refrescos naturales de Cuba...

Este remoto lugar de culta reunión, se nombraba "La Piña de Plata".

Hace más de cien años...

Actualmente—en el correr del tiempo—"La Piña de Plata" ha venido a nombrarse el Café "La Florida", que se asoma a la plazoleta de Albear, frente a las viejas rúas, cargadas con la tradición de un pasado de esplendor, lleno de majeza y heroísmo.

"La Piña de Plata" el café "La Florida", continúan, —uno en el recuerdo—el otro en la realidad de la diaria vida, sirviendo al público, hombres de negocios, políticos, profesionales, literatos y lindas mujeres elegantes, los finos batidos de frutas y los "cocktails" más delicados...

El bodegón "La Piña de Plata" se transformó al través de la intervención norteamericana en el cuartel general de los buenos catadores "yankees". Los "barmen" fueron poniendo una nota de modernidad en las simples bebidas primitivas y los claros esfuerzos de los hermanos Sala y el talento privilegiado de Constante han ido convirtiendo este rincón glorioso de la Habana en un refugio de arte y poesía.

Porque el "cocktail" moderno es la poesía del alcohol. Es como el perfume sutil de una flor... Es la esencia de una vibración y de una sensación deleitosa. El fino cristal de la copa del "cocktail", permite saborear la dura vida de una manera grata. El paisaje es más bello. El dolor es menos fuerte. El amor es más dulce y más tierno.

"Cocktail" es espiritualidad. "Grandes revistas norteamericanas e inglesas escribieron,—al comenzar en EE. UU. la Ley seca—que afortunadamente para las generaciones presentes, y futuras, el arte del "Cocktail" se conservaría—como la cultura antigua en Europa durante la invasión de los bárbaros, en dos templos sagrados. El "Bar American" de París frente a la Gran Opera, al fondo del Café de La Paix, y el Bar-Restaurant "La Florida", en la Habana, Cuba.

Ogaño—como hace un siglo—y sobre las viejas piedras de "La Piña de Plata", la Catedral del "cocktail" donde oficia Constante, se alza frente a las calles cargadas de tradición, para deleite de los buenos catadores y continúa siendo lugar predilecto, donde damas y caballeros saben esenciar los buenos vinos y sorber en éxtasis la quintaesencia perfumada de un "cocktail", símbolo dulce de una alta y laboriosa civilización.

"La Piña de Plata", el Café "La Florida". Año 1819-1935, al través de los siglos, siempre igual...

"Cocktail", Refrescos, Sorbetes, Sonrisas, Discreteos, Felicidad, Negocios, Esfuerzos, Amor... Sobre las mismas viejas piedras. Frente al mismo paisaje eterno. Bajo el mismo cielo cálido y azul.

L. F. M.

More than one hundred years ago — in the simple days of 1819 — a typical Spanish chophouse rose above the old city walls, at the entrance to Monserrate gate. It was a pleasant house of grilled windows that homed the beaux, the musicians, army officers, attorneys, actors, and men of all nature, people of honor and fashion desirous of the delicious, tasty "mixed gin" or cherry brandy.

In their carriages, the ladies, under their silken parasols, sipped — while being courted by their gallant knights — glasses of the various refreshments peculiar to Cuba.

This ideal, venerated place was named the "The Silver Pine".

¡Twas over a century ago!

At present—in the passage of time—"The Si'ver Pine" that faces Albear Square, overlooking the old colonial streets full of the traditions of a sp'endorous past of majestic heroism, has been renamed "La Florida".

"The Silver Pine" and "La Florida" cafe still stand—the former in our remembrance—the latter in the reality of life's daily toil, serving the public, business men, politicians, professionals, writers, and the most beautiful of e'egant women, with exquisite whipped fruit juices, and most delicate "cocktails".

"The Silver Pine" chophouse was tranformed during the days of the American occupation into a headquarters for the good Yankee tripplers. The bartenders gradually put o note of modernity in the simple drinks of our ancestors, and the valuable efforts of the Sala brot-

hers, added to the brigt talent and experiencie of Constante, have converted this glorious corner of Havana
into a refuge of Art and Poetry.

Because the modern "cocktail" is the poetry or liquor.

It is like the slender perfume of a rose. It is the
essence of a delicious vibration. The fine crystal of the
cocktail glass enables you to enjoy all the good that
exists, leaving the hardships of daily life forgotten. The
seenery is of unsurpassed beauty. Pain is unnoticeable.
Love is sweeter and more tender.

The "cocktail" is spiritualism!... Important magazi-
nes in the United States and England wrote — at the
beginning of the Dry Era — that, fortunately for the
present and future generations, the art of the cocktail
wou'd remain, as did ancient culture in Europe during
the invasión of the barbarians, safely revered in its most
sacred temples, viz; The American Bar in Paris, facing
the Grand Opera (at the rear of the Cafe de la Paix),
and the Bar Restaurant La Florida in Havana, Cuba.

Today, — as a Century ago — and situated over the
same old stones of "The Silver Pine", the Cathedral of
the Cocktail where Constante officiates stands amids the
streets of traditions for the delight of good drinkers and
continues to be the gathering place of men and women
who can distinguish the good wines and drink in extasy
the essence of a cocktail — sweet symbol of a high and
elaborate civilization.

"The Silver Pine", "La Florida" café — 1819-1935
— through the ages, always the same...
"Cocktails", Refreshments, Ices, Smiles, Flirtations,
Happiness, Business, fEforts, Love. Over the same old
stones. Facing the same scenary. Eternal, under the same warm blue sky.

"BACARDI"

FAMOUS SINCE 1838

"The rum that cured a King, and pickled a Nation".

Basil Woon

SANTIAGO DE CUBA - HABANA

Reach for

"HATUEY" beer instead...

Youl'll like it!
(Brewed by BACARDI)

COCKTAILS

A B C COCKTAIL

½ Vino de oporto.
½ Cognac fino.
1|3 Maraschino
1 Gota Angostura.
Varias ramas de hierba buena.
La corteza de un limón
½ Cucharadita de azúcar.
Hielo abundante en un vaso de 6 onzas.
Bátase ligeramente y sirvase sin colar con 2 guindas verdes.

½ Oporto Wine.
½ Fine Cognac.
1|3 Maraschino.
1 Dash angostura.
Several sprigs pepperpint.
Peel of a lemon.
½ Teaspoonful of sugar.
Plenty ice in a glass of 6 oz.
Shake a little and serve with 2 cherries.

ABSINTHE DROP
(French Style)

En una copa de 10 onzas.
¼ Anisette.
2 Onzas Absinthe Pernot
Hielo menudo en el colador.
Agua natural hasta llenarla.

Use a 10-ounces glass.

¼ Anisette.

2 Ounces Pernot Absinthe.

Cracked Ice in the strainer.

Fill glass to the brim with natural **water**.

ALEXANDER

1/3 Crema fresca leche.	1/3 Fresh Sweet Cream.
1/3 Gin Gordon.	1/3 Gordon Gin.
1/3 Crema Cacao.	1/3 Creme de Cacao.
1 Cucharadita de azúcar.	1 Teaspoonful Sugar.
La piel entera de un limón.	1 Full Lemon Peel.
Hielo menudo. Muy batido	Plenty of cracked ice.
y colado.	Shake well and strain into cocktail glass.

APERITAL COCKTAIL

2 Onzas Aperital Delor.	2 Ounces Aperital Delor.
La piel de un limón verde.	The peel of an unripe lemon.
1 Cucharadita Granadina.	1 Teaspoonful Grenadine.
Hielo abundante.	Cracked Ice.
Batido y sírvase sin colar.	Shake well and serve without straining.

BACARDI FLIP

1 Copa Ron Bacardí.	1 Glass Bacardi Rum.
	1 Spoonful Sugar.
1 Cucharada de azúcar.	1 Egg.
	Plenty Cracked Ice.
1 Huevo entero.	Shake well and strain; then, serve with powdered cinnamon on top.
Hielo menudo.	
Muy batido y sírvase colado y adornado con canela en polvo.	

"Cristal"

Beer

The

Best

BETWEEN-SHEETS

1/3 Cognac Tres Copas.	1/3 Tres Copas Cognac.
1/3 Crema Cacao.	1/3 Creme de Cacao.
1/3 Crema de leche fresca.	1/3 Fresh Sweet Cream.
1 Gota Angostura.	1 Dash Angostura.
1 Cucharadita de azúcar.	1 Teaspoonful Sugar.
La cáscara de un limón.	1 Lemon Peel.
Hielo abundante. Muy batido.	Plenty of Cracked ice. Shake well and strain into cocktail glass.

BLIND GEN

2 Yemas de huevos sin clara en una copa de Vino Moscatel o Vermouth Martini Rossi.	The Yolks of 2 Eggs. 1 Glass Moscatel Wine or Martini Rossi Vermouth.

BUTTERFLY
(Absinthe Frappe)

En una copa de 10 onzas con hielo menudo y abundante.	Use a 10-ounces glass.
Agua azucarada hasta casi llenarla.	Plenty of cracked ice.
2 Onzas Absinthe. Pernot flotando. Disuélvase lentamente con una cucharita hasta que se quede muy bien ligado.	Fill glass almost to the brim with sweetened water.
	2 Ounces Pernot Absinthe.
	Stir slowly with a spoon until well mixed; then drink.

BRANDY COCKTAIL

En un vaso de 10 onzas.	Use 10-ounces glass.
Hielo menudo.	Cracked Ice.
Una ramita hierba buena.	1 Sprig pepper-mint.
La cáscara de un limón verde con el jugo exprimido dentro.	1 Unripe Lemon Peel, squeezing juice in glass.
½ Cucharadita de azúcar.	½ Teaspoonful Sugar.
1 Gota Angostura.	1 Dash Angostura.
½ Cucharadita Curacao.	½ Teaspoonful Curacao.
2 Onzas Cognac Tres Copas	2 Ounces Tres Copas Cognac
Agítese de un vaso para el otro. Sirvase colado.	Shake lightly and strain; then, serve.

BRANDY FLIP

Copa Cognac Tres Copas.	1 Glass Tres Copas Cognac.
Cucharada de azúcar.	1 Spoonful Sugar.
Huevo entero.	1 Egg.
Hielo abundante.	Plenty cracked ice.
Muy batido y sírvase colado y adornado con canela en polvo.	Shake well and strain; then, serve with powdered cinnamon on top.

BRANDY COCKTAIL

2 Brandy (2 onzas).	2 Ounces Brandy.
1 Gota de Angostura.	1 Dash Angostura Bitters.
½ Cucharadita de Curacao.	½ Teaspoonful Curacao.
1 Ramita hierba buena.	1 Small Sprig of Pepper mint.
Cáscara limón con su jugo.	½ Teaspoonful.
½ Cucharadita de azúcar.	Sugar.
Batido y colado.	1 Lemon Peel.
1 Small Sprig of Pepper-mint.	Shake well and strain.

MANZANILLA
OLOROSA

CREADO POR

Comp. MATA

UNION DE BODEGAS ANDALUZAS,
S. A.

MARCA INTERNACIONAL, NUM. 33068

VINO FINO DE
SANLÚCAR

Representante:
Romualdo Lalueza,
TELEFONO A-2025

. 411

BRANDY DAISSY

Una copa llena de hielo menudo.	A glass full of cracked ice.
1 gota Angostura.	1 Dash Angostura.
½ Cucharadita de Chatreusse amarillo.	½ Teaspoonful Yellow Chartreuse.
2 Onzas Cognac Tres Copas.	2 Ounces Tres Copas Cognac.
½ Cáscara limón verde y jugo.	½ Lemon Peel. A few sprigs pepper-mint.
Unas ramitas hierba buena.	2 Cherries.
Dos guindas. Sírvase sin colar.	Stir and serve without straining.

BRONX

1/3 Vermouth Martini Rossi	1/3 Vermouth Martini Rossi
1/3 Vermouth Nolly Prat.	1/3 Nolly Prat Vermouth.
1/3 Gin Gordon.	1/3 Gordon Gin.
1/2 Cucharadita Curacao.	1/2 Teaspoonful Curacao.
1 Cucharadita jugo naranja.	1 Teaspoonful Orange Juice.
Hielo menudo. Ligeramente batido y colado.	Cracked ice. Shake lightly and strain; then, serve.

BRONX NUM. 2
(F.oridita Style)

1/3 Vermouth Nolly Prat.	1/3 Nolly Prat Vermouth.
1/3 Vermouth Martini Rossi	1/3 Martini Rossi Vermouth
1/3 Gin Gordon.	1/3 Gordon Gin.
1/2 Cucharadita Curacao.	1/2 Teaspoonful Curacao.
Hielo menudo. Enfríese sin batirlo y cuélese. Sírvase con una piel de naranja y dos guindas.	Cracked ice. Do not shake. Strain and serve very cold with a lemon peel and two cherries.

BLUE PARADISE

½ Dubonnet.
½ Cognac Tres Copas.
1/3 Perfait Amour.
La cáscara de un limón.
Hielo menudo. Batido y colado.

½ Dubonnet.
½ Tres Copas Cognac.
1/3 Perfait Amour.
1 Lemon Peel.
Cracked Ice.
Shake well and strain into
cocktail glass.

BLUE MOON

½ Crema Violeta.
½ Cognac Tres Copas.
½ Cucharadita Menta verde
Hielo abundante. Batido y
colado.

½ Creme de Violete.
½ Tres Copas Cognac.
1 Teaspoonful Green Cre-
me de Menthe.
Plenty of cracked ice.
Shake well and strain into
a cocktail glass.

CAFFERY SPECIAL COCKTAIL

2 Oz. Sloe Gin.
1 Cucharadita de jugo
de naranja.
1 Cucharadita de Apri-
cot Brandy.
½ Cucharadita de jara-
be Granadina Hielo
abundante. En una co-
pa de forma cónica de 6
onzas, adornado con
lascas de piña y 2
guindas.

1|3 2 oz. Sloe Gin.
1 Teaspoonful o r a n-
ge juice .
1 Teaspoonful Apricot
Brandy.
½ Teaspoonful Granadine
Sirup.
Plenty ice. In a co-
nic glass of 6 oz.
Serve with slices of
pineapple and 2 che-
rries.

CLEOPATRA

½ Vino Oporto.	½ Port Wine.
½ Cognac Tres Copas.	½ Tres Copas Cognac.
1/3 Cointreau.	1/3 Cointreau.
1/3 Jugo de piña.	1/3 Pineapple Juice.
Hielo menudo. Batido y colado.	Cracked Ice.
	Shake well and strain into cocktail glass.

CASIANO COCKTAIL

2 Onzas de Vermouth Martini Rossi.	2 Ounces Martini Rossi Vermouth.
1 Cucharada Crema Cassis.	1 Teaspoonful Creme Cassis.
La piel de un limón.	1 Lemon Peel.
Hielo menudo.	Cracked Ice.
Batido y colado.	Shake and strain then, serve.

CALEDONIA
(Special)

1/3 Crema Cacao.	1/3 Creme de Cacao.
1/3 Cognac Tres Copas.	1/3 Tres Copas Cognac.
1/3 Leche fresca.	1/3 Fresh sweet milk.
1 Gota Angostura.	The Yolk of 1 Egg.
1 Yema de huevo.	1 Dash Angostura.
La Cáscara de un limón.	1 Lemon Peel.
Hielo menudo. Batido y colado. Adórnese con canela.	Crushed Ice.
	Shake well and strain. Serve in cocktail glass with Cinnamon on top.

CAFE COCKTAIL

1 Café puro.	1 Black Coffee.
½ Crema Cacao.	½ Creme de Cacao.
½ Cognac Soberano.	½ Soberano Cognac.
1 Cucharadita azúcar.	1 Teaspoonful Sugar.
La cáscara de un limón.	1 Lemon Peel.
Hielo menudo. Batido y co-lado.	Cracked Ice.
	Shake well and strain into cocktail glass.

CLOVER CLUB

2 Onzas Gin Gordon.	2 Ounces Gordon Gin.
Varias gotas Menta blanca.	Several Dashes White Mint.
El jugo de ½ limón verde.	The Juice of ½ Lemon.
1 Cucharadita Granadina.	1 Teaspoonful Grenedine.
Hielo menudo. Bien batido y	Plenty of Cracked Ice.
La clara de un huevo.	The White of 1 Egg.
colado.	Shake well and strain into cocktail glass.

DAIQUIRI NUM. 1

2 Onzas Ron Bacardí.	2 Ounces Bacardí Rum.
	1 Teaspoonful Sugar.
1 Cucharadita de azúcar	Juice of half a lemon.
	Cracked ice.
Jugo de 1|2 limón verde.	Shake well and strain into cocktail glass.
Hielo menudito.	
Bátase perfectamente y cuélese.	

DAIQUIRI NUM. 2

2 Onzas Ron Bacardi.	2 Ounces Bacardí Rum.
Unas gotas de Curacao.	Several Dashes Curacao.
1 Cucharadita jugo naranja.	1 Teaspoonful Orange Juice.
1 Cucharadita de azúcar.	1 Teaspoonful Sugar.
El jugo de 1:2 limón.	Juice of Half a Lemon.
Hielo menud to.	Cracked ice.
Batido y colado.	Shake well and strain into cocktail glass.

DAIQUIRI NUM. 3
(B. Orbon)

2 Onzas Ron Bacardí.	2 Ounces Bacardí Rum.
1 Cucharada de azúcar.	1 Spoonful Sugar.
1 Cucharadita jugo de toronja.	1 Teaspoonful Grape Fruit Juice.
1 Cucharadita Marraschino.	1 Teaspoonful Marraschino.
Jugo de 112 limón verde.	Juice of half a lemon.
Hielo frappe.	Shake well and strain into
Batido y sírvase frappe.	cocktail glass. Serve frappe.

DAIQUIRI NUM. 4
(Florida Style)

2 Onzas Ron Bacardí.	2 Ounces Bacardí Rum.
1 Cucharadita de azúcar.	1 Teaspoonful Sugar.
1 Cucharadita Marraschino.	1 Teaspoonful Marraschino.
Jugo de 1!2 limón verde.	Juice of half a lemon.
Batido e'éctricamente con hielo afeitado. Sírvase frappe.	Shake in an electric shaker with crushed ice. Serve frappe.

DIAMOND HITCH

En un vaso de 12 onzas.	Use a 10-ounces glass.
2 Onzas Ginebra.	2 Ounces Gin.
1 Gota Angostura.	1 Dash Angostura.
Piel de un limón.	1 Lemon Peel.
Hielo menudo.	Plenty Cracked Ice.
Champagne hasta llenarlo sin colar.	Fill glass to the brim with Champagne.
	Do not strain.

DELIO NUÑEZ

1/3 Jugo Toronja.	1/3 Grape Fruit Juice.
½ Gin Gordon.	½ Gordon Gin.
½ Cucharadita azúcar.	½ Teaspoonful Sugar.
1 Cucharadita Marraschino.	1 Teaspoonful Marraschino
½ Clara de huevo.	Shake well and strain into
Hielo menudo. Muy batido y colado.	Half of the white of an egg. cocktail glass.

EUREKA

½ Sloe Gin Gallo.	½ Gordon's Sloe Gallo.
½ Calvados.	½ Calvados.
1 Cucharadita de jugo de limón.	1 Teaspoonful Sherry Brandy.
1 Cucharadita Sherry Brandy.	1 Teaspoonful Lemon Juice.
Hielo menudo. Batido y colado.	Cracked Ice. Shake well and strain into cocktail glass.

EGG-NOG

1 Cucharada de azúcar.	1 Spoonful Sugar.
2 Onzas Cognac Tres Copas.	2 Ounces Tres Copas Cognac
6 Onzas leche fresca.	6 Ounces Fresh Milk.
Hielo Batido y colado.	2 Eggs.
Adornado con canela en polvo. Uno o dos huevos adentro.	Cracked Ice. Shake well and strain; then, serve.

FLORIDITA SPECIAL

1/3 Rye Whiskey.	1/3 Rye Whisky.
½ Vermouth Martini Rossi.	½ Martini Rossi Vermouth.
1 Cucharadita Amer Picón.	1 Teaspoonful Amer Picon.
½ Cucharadita Curacao.	½ Teaspoonful Curacao.
½ Cucharadita azúcar.	½ Teaspoonful Sugar.
1 Gota Angostura.	1 Dash Angostura.
1 Cáscara pequeña de limón	1 Small Lemon Peel.
Hielo menudo. Batido y colado.	Cracked ice. Shake well and strain into cocktail glass.

GIN FIZZ

2 Onzas Gin Gordon.	2 Ounces Gordon Gin.
1 Cucharadita azúcar.	1 Teaspoonful Sugar.
Jugo de ½ limón.	The Juice of ½ Lemon.
Varias gotas Menta blanca.	Several Dashes of white
Hielo menudo. Muy batido y después de colado agréguese un poco de agua de Seltz.	Creme de Menthe. Crushed ice. Shake very well and strain; then add some Seltz water. Serve.

GIN COCKTAIL

En un vaso de 10 onzas.
Hielo menudo.
Una ramita hierba buena.
La cáscara de un limón
verde con el jugo exprimido dentro.
½ Cucharadita de azúcar.
1 Gota Angostura.
½ Cucharadita Curacao.
2 Onzas Gin Gordon.
Agítese de un vaso para el
otro. Sírvase colado.

Use a 10-ounces glass.
Cracked Ice.
1 Sprig pepper-mint.
1 Unripe Lemon Pcel,
Squeezing juice in glass.
½ Teaspoonful Sugar.
1 Dash Angostura.
½ Teaspoonful Curacao.
2 Ounces Gordon Gin.
Shake lightly and strain;
then, serve.

GIN DAISSY

1 copa llena de hielo me-
nudo.

½ Cáscara limón verde con
jugo.

1 Gota Angostura.

½ Cucharadita de Chatreu-
sse amarillo.

2 Onzas Gin Gordon.

½ Cucharadita azúcar.

4 Ramitas hierba buena.

1 Guinda encima.

Sírvase sin colar.

Take a glass and fill it
with cracked ice; then put
in:
½ Unsqueezed Lemon Peel.
1 Dash Angostura.
½ Teaspoonful Yellow
Chartleuse.
2 Ounces Gordon Gin.
½ Teaspoonful Sugar.
4 Sprigs Pepper-mint.
1 Cherry on top.
Stir and serve without straining.

El agua
predilecta
de la sociedad

Agua mineral
San Agustín

GOLDEN GATE

(Ideal para disipar en breves minutos los efectos del exceso alcohólico y poder continuar hasta lo infinito).

(Ideal to take off in a few minutes the efects of the alcohol and to be able to go along till the infinite).

En un vaso de 10 onzas póngase hielo menudo y abundante.

In a glass of 10 oz. put plenty crushed ice.

El jugo de 2 limones.

The juice of 2 lemons.

Una cucharada de almíbar natural.

1 Spoonful of simple sirup

Una cucharadita de bicarbonato.

1 Teaspoonful of bicarbonate.

Agua natural hasta llenarlo.

Fill glass with spring water.

Bébase mientras está en efervecencia.

Drink while in effervescence.

GOLDEN GLOVE

2 Onzas Ron Jamaica.

2 Ounces Jamaica Rum.

1 Cucharadita Cointreau.

1 Teaspoonful Cointreau.

1 Cucharadita azúcar.

1 Teaspoonful Sugar.

Jugo de ½ limón verde.

The Juice of ½ Lemon.

Hielo frappe. Batido eléctricamente. Sírvase frappe después de exprimirle encima una cáscara de naranja.

Crushed Ice.
Shake in electrical shaker. Serve frappe after squeezing into it an orange peel.

GOLDEN DAWN

½ Calvados App'e Jack.
½ Gin Gordon.
1/3 Apricot Brandy.
½ Cucharadita Granadina.
1 Cucharadita jugo na-
ranja.
Hielo menudo. Batido y colado. Sirvase con una guinda.

½ Calvados or Applejack.
½ Gordon Gin.
1/3 Apricot Brandy.
½ Teaspoonful Grenadine.
1 Teaspoonful Orange
Juice.
Cracked Ice.
Shake well and strain. Serve
in cocktail glass with one
cherry.

GOLDEN FIZZ

2 Onzas Gin Gordon.
1 Cucharadita de azúcar.
½ Cucharadita de Curacao.
Jugo de ½ limón.
La yema de un huevo.
Hielo abundante. Muy batido y colado.

2 Ounces Gordon Gin.
1 Teaspoonful Sugar.
½ Teaspoonful Curacao.
The Juice or ½ Lemon.
The York of 1 Egg.
Plenty of cracked ice.
Shake well and strain into
glass.

GREEN FIZZ

2 Onzas Gin Gordon.
1 Cucharadita de azúcar.
1 Cucharadita Menta verde
Jugo de ½ limón.
1 Clara de huevo.
Hielo menudo. Muy batido y
colado.

2 Ounces Gordon Gin.
1 Teaspoonful Sugar.
1 Teaspoonful Green Mint.
The Juice of half a lemon.
The White of 1 Egg.
Cracked Ice.
Shake well and strain. Them
serve.

HAVANA BEACH
(Special)

½ Jugo piña.
½ Ron Bacardí.
1 Cucharadita azúcar.
Muy batido con hielo menudo. Sírvase colado.

½ Pineapple Juice.
½ Bacardí Rum.
1 Teaspoonful Sugar.
Cracked Ice.
Shake well and strain into cocktail glass.

HOT-KISS

½ Cognac Soberano.
½ Vermouth Martín Rossi.
1 Cucharadita Curacao.
Enfríese sin batirlo y colado.
Sírvase con un par de guindas.

½ Soberano Cognac.
½ Martín Rossi Vermouth.
1 Teaspoonful Curacao.
Do not shake. Strain and serve cold with two cherries.

CHAPARRA

½ Ron Bacardí.

½ Vermouth Martini Rossi.

La cáscara de un limón verde mien estrujada con el hielo.

½ Cucharadita azúcar.

Enfríese sin batirlo, y cuélese dejando el limón en forma espiral en la copa.

½ Bacardi Rum.
½ Martini Rossi Vermouth.
½ Teaspoonful Sugar.
1 Lemon Peel thoroughly squeezed.
Do not shake. Strain and serve very cold leaving lemon peel in glass in the shape of a spiral.

CHAMPAGNE COCKTAIL

En una copa flouriforme de 10 onzas, llena de hielo menudo, póngase:
1 Terrón de azúcar.
1 Ramita hierba buena.
La piel de un limón.
Llénese con Champagne y adórnese con guindas.

In a 10-ounces glass filled with cracked ice put:
1 Lump of sugar.
1 Sprig pepper-mint.
1 Lemon peel.
Fill the glass to the brim with Champagne and decorate with cherries.

CHAMPAGNE PUNCH
100 Glasses

2½ Libras azúcar.
2 Onzas Angostura.
1 Nuez Moscada y molida.
1 Piña blanca cortada menudita.
4 Melocotones cortados menuditos.
½ Pomo de guindas.
Corteza de dos limones.
Corteza de dos naranjas.
1 Botella crema de cacao.
1 Botella Apricot Brandy.
1 Botella de Cognac fino.
6 Botellas de Champagne.
6 Botellas de vino blanco.
En una ponchera con hielo y sal. granada exteriormente.

2½ Pound of sugar.
2 Oz. Angostura.
1 Nutmeg pounden.
1 White pineapple small slices.
4 Peaches cuted small pieces.
½ Bottle of Cherris.
Peel of 2 lemons.
Peel of 2 oranges.
1 Botted Creme de Cacao.
1 Bottle Apricot Brandy.
1 Bottle Fine Cognac.
6 Bottles Champagne.
6 Bottles White Wine.
In one Punch - bowl with ice and salt outward.

CHAPARRON

2/3 Cognac Tres Copas.
1/3 Vermouth Martini Rossi
La cáscara de un limón completo en espiral en la copa.
½ Cucharadita de azúcar.
Bien mojada la piel del limón con el azúcar para que quede bien saturada de su perfume. Enfríese y cuélese. Sirvase con la piel dentro de la copa.

2/3 Tres Copas Cognac.
1/3 Martini Rossi Vermouth
½ Teaspoonful Sugar.
1 Lemon Peel forming a spiral.
Thoroughly mix lemon peel with sugar so as to saturate the concoction with the perfum of the lemon. Strain and serve very cold with the lemon peel in the g'ass.

CHANTECLAIR

½ Cognac Soberano.
½ Vermouth Ama.
1 Cucharadita Curacao.
Enfríese y cuálese sin batir. Sirvase y cuélese con dos guindas.

½ Soberano Cognac.
½ Ama Vermouth.
1 Teaspoonful Curacao.
Do not shake. Strain and serve iced with two cherries.

CHIC

¼ Jugo Toronja.
½ Vermouth Martini Rossi.
½ Sloe Gin Gordon.
1 Cucharadita Marraschino
Hie o menudo. Muy batido y colado. Sirvase con varias almendras.

¼ Grape Fruit.
½ Martini Rossi Vermouth.
½ Gordon's Sloe Gin.
1 Teaspoonful Marraschino
Cracked ice.
Shake very well and strain into cocktail glass. Serve with a few almonds.

VERMOUTH · TORINO

BROCCHI

MARTINI · & ROSSI

único

para

cocktails

JABON CANDADO
(Ramoncito López Especial)

2 Onzas Ron Bacardí.
1 Cucharadita de azúcar.
Jugo de 1|2 limón verde.
½ Clara de huevo.
Hielo menudo. Bien batido y colado.

2 Ounces Bacardí Rum.
1 Teaspoonful Sugar.
Juice of half a lemon.
½ of the white of an egg.
Cracked ice.
Shake well and strain into a cocktail glass.

IDEAL

¼ Toronja.
1 Cucharadita Marraschino
1/3 Vermouth Martini Rossi
1/3 Vermouth Nolly Prat.
1/3 Gin Gordon.
Hielo menudo. Muy batido y colado. Sírvase con varias almendras.

¼ Grape Fruit.
1 Teaspoonful Marraschino
1/3 Martini Rossi Vermouth.
1/3 Nolly Prat Vermouth.
1/3 Gordon Gin.
Cracked ice.
Shake very well and strain into cocktail glass. Serve with a few almonds.

JOSEPHINE BAKER

1|2 Cognac Soberano.
1|2 Vino Oporto.
1|3 Apricot Brandy.
1 Cucharadita de azúcar, la cáscara de un limón, la yema de un huevo, hielo menudito.
Bien batido y colado. Canela por arriba.

1|2 Soberano Cognac.
1|2 Port Wine.
1|3 Apricot Brandy.
1 Teaspoonful Sugar.
1 Lemon Peel.
Yolk of an egg.
Cracked ice.
Shake well and strain into cocktail glass. Cinnamon on top.

LONGINES COCKTAIL

1/3 Cognac Soberano.	1/3 Soberano Cognac.
1/3 Anís del Mono.	1/3 Anis del Mono.
1/3 Té fuerte.	1/3 Harsh The.
La piel de un limón.	Peel of a lemon.
1 Cucharadita de azúcar.	1 Teaspoonful of sugar.
Hielo abundante, bien batido y colado.	Plenty ice, shake well and strain.

MARY PICKFORD

½ Jugo Piña.	½ Pine-apple Juice.
½ Ron Bacardí.	½ Bacardi Rum.
½ Cucharadita Granadina	½ Teaspoonful Grenedine.
Hielo menudo. Batido y colado.	Crushed Ice. Shake well and strain into cocktail glass.

MANHATTAN
(Seco)

½ Vermouth Nolly Prat.	½ Nolly Prat Vermouth.
½ Rye Whiskey.	½ Rye Whiskey.
1 Gota Angostura.	1 Dash Angostura.
Hielo menudo. Enfríese sin batirlo y cuélese.	Cracked Ice. Do not shake. Let it become very cold, strain and serve.

MANHATTAN
(Medio Dulce)

½ Vermouth Martini Rossi.	½ Martini Rossi Vermouth.
½ Rye Whisky.	½ Rye Whisky.
1 Gota Angostura.	1 Dash Angostura.
Hielo menudo. Enfríese sin batirlo y cuélese.	Cracked Ice. Do not shake. Let it become very cold, strain and serve.

MANHATTAN
(Dulce)

½ Vermouth Martini Rossi.
½ Rye Whiskey.
½ Cucharadita de Curacao.
Hielo menudo. Enfríese sin
batirlo y cuélese. Sírvase con
dos guindas.

½ Martini Rossi Vermouth.
½ Rye Whisky.
½ Teaspoonful Curacao.
Cracked Ice.
Do not shake. Let it get
very cold and strain.
Serve with two cherries.

MARTINI
(Seco)

½ Gin Gordon.
½ Vermouth Nolly Prat.
2 Gotas Orange Bitter.
Hielo menudo. Enfríese sin
batirlo y cuélese. Sírvase con
una aceituna.

½ Gordon Gin.
½ Nolly Prat Vermouth.
2 Dashes Orange Bitter.
Cracked Ice.
Do not shake. Ollow it to
get very cold and strain.
Serve with an olive.

MARTINI
(Demi-seco)

½ Gin Gordon.
½ Vermouth Nolly Prat.
2 Gotas Orange Bitter.
Hielo menudo. Enfríese sin
batirlo y cuélese.

½ Gordon Gin.

½ Nolly Prat Vermouth.

2 Dashes Orange Bitter.

Cracked Ice.

Do not shake. Allow it to
get very cold and strain.
Then serve.

MARCO-ANTONIO

1/3 Jugo de toronja.
1 Cucharadita Marraschino.
2 Onzas Gin Gordon.
1 Cucharadita Granadina.
½ Clara huevo.
Hielo menudo. Batido y colado.

1/3 Grape Fruit Juice.
1 Teaspoonful Marraschino.
2 Ounces Gordon Gin.
1 Teaspoounful Grenadine.
½ The white of an egg.
Cracked Ice.
Shake well and strain into cocktail glass.

MARY MORANDEYRA

1/3 Jugo Toronja.
1/3 Sloe Gin Gordon. Rossi.
1 Cucharadita Marraschino.
Hielo abundante menudo.
Colado.

1/3 Grape Fruit Juice.
1 3 Gordon Sloe Gin.
1/3 Martini Rossi Vermouth.
1 Teaspoonful Marraschino.
Plenty cracked ice, and strain it into a glass.

MENDEZ VIGO-SPECIAL

2 Onzas Cognac Tres Copas.
1 Cucharadita azúcar.
1 Cucharadita Marraschino.
Jugo de ½ limón verde.
Hielo frappe. Batido eléctricamente. Sírvase frappe.

2 Ounce Cognac Tres Copas
1 Teaspoonful Sugar.
1 Teaspoonful Marraschino.
The Juice of ½ lemon.
Shake in electric shacker and serve frappe.

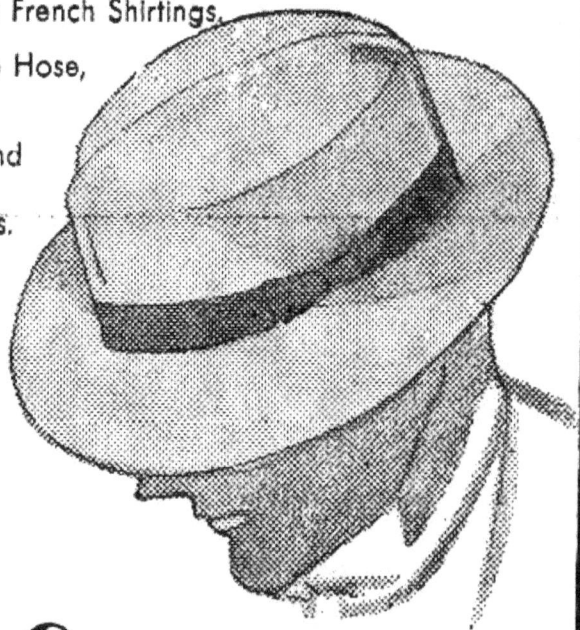

MENDIETA SPECIAL COCKTAIL

1'3 Vermouth italiano.
1;3 Vermouth N. Prat.
1 3 Old Tom Gin.
1;2 Cucharadita de cura-
zao
Hielo menudo. Enfrie-
se perfectamente y
cuéiese. Sirvase con
dos guindas y corteza
de naranja.

1 3 Italian Vermouth.
1 3 N. Prat Vermouth.
1 3 Old Tom Gin
1 3 Teaspoonful of Cura-
cao Crushed ice

Strain and serve ice
with 2 cherries and peel
of orange.

MENT-JULEP
(Mexican Style)

En un vaso de old fashion
lleno de hielo menudo y con
hierba buena abundante.

1 Cáscara de limón.

1 Cucharadita Marraschino

½ Vino Oporto.

½ Cognac Soberano.

1 Gota Angostura.

½ Cucharadita azúcar.

Agitese violentamente y sírvase con dos guindas y sin
colar

1 Old-fashioned glass full
ice and plenty of pepper-
mint.
1 Lemon Peel.
1 Teaspoonful Marraschino
½ Port Wine.
½ Soberano Cognac.
1 Dash Angostura.
½ Teaspoonful Sugar.
Shake well. Serve with 2
cherries.

MISS JOAN KETCHUM SPECIAL COCKTAIL

½ Jugo de piña.	½ Pineapple juice.
½ Old Tom. Gin.	½ Old Tom Gin.
1 Cucharadita de Apricot Brandy.	1 Teaspoonful Apricot Brandy.
1 Cucharadita de Jarabe de granadina.	1 Teaspoonful Granadine sirup.
Hielo menudo, batido y colado.	Shake well and strain Crushed ice.

MY-SIN COCKTAIL
(Manolo Solis Mendieta)

1 Onza Ajenjo.	1 Oz. Abshente.
1 Gota Angostura.	1 Oz. Anisette.
½ Clara de huevo.	1 Drop Angostura.
	½ White of an egg.
Hielo abundante, bien batido y colado.	Plenty ice, shake well and strain.
Humedézcase el borde del vaso con jugo de limón y azúcar en polvo.	Wet the glass edge with lemon juice and dust sugar.

MONO COCKTAIL

2 Onzas Anis del Mono.	2 Ounces Anis del Mono.
1 Onza Angostura.	1 Drop Angostura.
Hielo abundante, bien batido y colado.	Plenty ice. Shake well, strain and serve.

MOFUCO COCKTAIL

2 Onz. Ron Bacardí.	2 Oz. Bacardí Run.
L acorteza de un limón.	1 Peel of a lemon.
Una cucharadita de azúcar	1 Teaspunful of sugar.
Una gota de angostura bitters.	1 Drop Angostura bitters.
Un huevo entero.	1 All egg.
Bátase perfectamente con hielo abundante y cuélese.	Shake very well with plenty ice and strain.

MORNING STAR

½ Vino Oporto.	½ Port Wine.
½ Cognac Soberano.	½ Soberano Cognac.
1 Gota Angostura.	1 Dash Angostura.
1 Cucharadita azúcar.	1 Teaspoonful Sugar.
1 Huevo entero.	1 Egg.
Hielo abundante.	Plenty Cracked Ice.
Muy batido. Sírvase colado y adornado con canela en polvo.	Shake well and strain into glass. Put some powdered cinnamon on top.

MIAMI BEACH
(Special)

½ Jugo piña.	½ Pineapple Juice.
½ Gin Gordon.	½ Gordon Gin.
1 Cucharadita azúcar.	1 Teaspoonful Sugar.
Hielo menudo. Batido y colado.	Cracked Ice. Shake well and strain into cocktail glass.

HAY MUCHOS RONES, PERO SOLO UN BACARDI

42

MOJITO CRIOLLO

En un vaso de 8 onzas. Hielo menudo. Varias ramitas hierba buena, la cáscara de un limón con el jugo exprimido dentro. 1 Cucharadita de azúcar. 2 Onzas Ron Bacardí. Agitese con una cuchara pajugo. Agréguese agua carra que la hierba suelte el bonatada y sirvase sin colar.

Use 8-ounces glass. Cracked Ice. Several sprigs pepper-mint. 1 Lemon Peel, squeezing juice into glass. 1 Teaspoonful Sugar. 2 Onces Bacardi Rum. Stir with a spoon. Add sparkling water and serve without straining.

MOJITO CRIOLLO Nº 2

En un vaso de 8 onzas.

Hielo menudo.

Varias ramitas hierba buena.

La cáscara de un limón con el jugo exprimido dentro.

1 Cucharadita de azúcar.

2 Onzas Cinebra Gordon.

Agitese con la cuchara para que la hierba suelte el jugo. Agréguese agua carbonatada y sirva sin colar.

Use 8-ounces glass. Cracked Ice. Several sprigs pepper-mint. 1 Lemon Peel, squeezing juice into glass. 1 Teaspoonful Sugar. 2 Ounces Gordon's Gin. Stir with spoon. Add sparkling water and serve without straining.

44

MINT-JULEP
(Virginia Style)

Hierba buena abundante.	Plenty of Pepper-mint.
1 Cucharadita de azúcar.	1 Teaspoonful Sugar.
Estrújese bien la hierba buena con el azúcar.	Thoroughly mix pepper-mint with sugar.
2 Onzas Rey Whiskey.	2 Ounces Rey Whisky.
2 Gotas de limón.	2 Drops Lemon Juice.
Sírvase en un vaso lleno de hielo menudo y adornado con varias ramitas de hierba buena y una guinda.	Serve in a glass with plenty of cracked ice, decorated with small branches of pepper-mint and one cherry.

NATIONAL COCKTAIL

¼ Apricot Brandy.	¼ Apricot Brandy.
¼ Jugo piña.	¼ Pine-apple Juice.
½ Ron Bacardí.	½ Bacardí Rum.
Hielo menudo.	Cracked Ice.
Batido y colado.	Shake well and strain in cocktail glass.
Adórnese con lascas de piña y guindas.	Decorate glass with slices of pine-apple and cherries.

PARIS MIDI

En una copa de 10 onzas.	Use a 10-ounces glass.
Hielo menudo.	Cracked Ice.
1/3 Crema Cassis.	1/3 Creme Cassis.
2/3 Vermouth Nolly Prat.	2/3 Nolly Prat Vermouth.
Agua carbonatada.	Sparkling water.
Agítese con una cucharita y sírvase.	Stir with a spoon and serve.

MOJITO CRIOLLO Nº 3

En un vaso de 8 onzas.	Use 8-ounces glass.
Hielo menudo.	Cracked Ice.
Varias ramitas hierba buena.	Several sprigs pepper-mint.
La cáscara de un limón verde con el jugo exprimido dentro del vaso.	1 Lemon Peel, squeezing juice into glass.
2 Onzas Cognac Soberano.	2 Ounceas Soberano Cognac
1 Cucharadita de azúcar.	1 Teaspoonful Sugar.
Agítese con la cuchara para que la hierba suelte el jugo. Agréguese agua carbonatada y sirva sin colar.	Stir with spoon. Add sparkling water and serve without straining.

MONJITA

En una copa de 6 onzas.	Use a 10-ounce glass.
Hielo menudo.	Cracked Ice.
½ Agua carbonatada.	½ Sparkling Water.
½ Anís del Mono (seco o dulce).	½ Anís del Mono either dry or sweet).

MC AVOY
(Special)

½ Vainilla ice cream. ½ Cognac Soberano. Batido y colado. Adórnese con caneda en polvo.	½ Vainilla Ice-cream. ½ Soberano Cognac. Shake and strain; serve with powdered cinnamon on top.

If you want to have your table nicely set, you need only to get some fine crockery and crystal. For that purpose call on

"La América"

LOCERIA FINA
Galiano Nº 113

the well known crockery store in **Galiano Nº 113**, where they have an excellent exposition of the most exquisite Sajonia and Limoges porcelain. The same in crystal Val Saint Lambert, St. Luis, cut-glass, etc., We now have special prices ond all merchandise.

PICK-ME-UP

½ Dobonnet.	½ Dobonnet.
½ Cognac Soberano.	½ Soberano Cognac.
1/3 Anisette.	1/3 Anisette.
1 Cáscara de limón.	1 Lemon Peel.
½ Clara de huevo.	½ The white of an egg.
Hielo menudo. Batido y colado.	Cracked Ice.
	Shake well and strain into a cocktail glass.

PORTO FLIP

1 Copa Vino Oporto.	1 Glass Port Wine.
1 Cucharada de azúcar.	1 Spoonful Sugar.
1 Huevo entero.	1 Egg.
Hielo abundante.	Plenty cracked ice.
Muy batido y sírvase colado y adornado con canela en polvo.	Shake well and strain; then, serve with powdered cinnamon on top.

POUSSE CAFE

1|2 Cognac Tres Copas	1|2 Tres copas Cognac.
1|3 Anissette	1|3 Anisette.
1|3 Crema Cacao	1|3 Creme de Cacao.
1 Cucharadita de Café puro.	1 Teaspoonful Back Coffee.
Enfríese y sírvase sin hielo	Serve cold without ice.

PRESIDENTE COCKTAIL

½ Vermouth Chambery.
½ Bacardí Oro.
½ Cucharadita de Curacao.
Hielo menudo.
Enfríese perfectamente y cuélese.
Sírvase con guindas y una corteza de naranja.

½ Chambery Bermouth
½ Bacardí Gold.
½ Teaspoonful of Curacao.
Crushed ice.
Cool well and strain.
Serve with cherries and a peel of orange.

PRESIDENTE MENOCAL SPECIAL

En un vaso de 8 onzas póngase hierba buena abundante.

Una cucharadita de azúcar.

Varias gotas de limón.

Estrújese bien la hierba buena.

2 onzas de Bacardí.

Llénese el vaso de hielo menudo y adórnese con un ramito de yerba buena entero y dos guindas.

In a glass of 8 oz. put plenty of Pepper-mint.

1 Teaspoonful of sugar. Several drops of Lemon juice crush the Pepper-mint.

2 Oz. Bacardi.

Fill glass with crushed ice; serve with Pepper-mint and 2 cherries.

PLANTERS-PUNCH

Una copa de las usadas parara champagne. Llena de hielo.	Take a glass and fill it with cracked ice. Then put in:
Jugo de ½ limón.	The Juice of ½ Lemon.
1 Cucharadita de Curacao.	1 Teaspoonful Curacao.
1 Cucharadita Granadina.	1 Teaspoonful Grenadine.
2 Onzas Ron Jamaica.	2 Ounces Jamaica Rum.
Sírvase sin colar, adornado de lascas de piña, naranja y limón.	Serve without straining in glass decorated with slices of pineapple, orange and Lemon.

RAMOS GIN FIZZ

2 Onzas Gin Gordon.	The Juice of ½ Lemon.
El jugo de ½ limón.	2 Ounces Gordon Gin.
1 Cucharadita jarabe almendras.	1 Teaspoonful Almond Sirup
1 Cucharadita agua de azahar.	1 Teaspoonful Orange-flower Water.
½ Onza crema fresca.	½ Ounce Fresh Cream.
Bien batido y colado.	Shake well and strain in cocktail glass.

50

RAIN BOW
(After dinner drik)

Insuperable.
Chartreuse.
Curacao.
Marraschino.
Parfait Amour.
Peppermint.
Cacao.
Póngase muy despacio en una copa alta, empezando por el último o sea el Cacao.

Insuperable.
Chartreuse.
Curacao.
Marraschino.
Parfait Amour.
Pepper-mint.
Cacao.
Pour very slow'y into a long glass, starting with the last, namely, the cacao.

"REX"
(Special)

En una copa de 10 onzas.
Hie'o menudo.
La p'el de un limón francés.
¼ Bitter Solamer.
¾ Vermouth Martini Rossi.
Agua carbonatada.
Sírvase sin colar.

Use a 10-ounces glass.
Cracked Ice.
The peel of a French 'emon.
¼ Bitters.
¾ Martini Rossi Vermouth.
Sparkling Water.
Serve without straining.

ROYAL FIZZ

2 Onzas Gin Gordon.
1 Cucharadita de azúcar.
½ Cucharadita de Curacao.
Jugo de ½ limón verde.
1 Huevo completo.
Hie'o menudo. Muy batido y colado.

2 Ounces Gordon Gin.
1 Teaspoonful Sugar.
½ Teaspoonful Curacao.
The uice of ½ Unripe Lemon
1 Egg (the white and the yolk).
Cracked ice.
Shake well and strain. Then serve.

PEPIN RIVERO
(Special)

1/3 Crema Cacao.
1/3 Gin Gordon.
1/3 Leche fresca.
1/6 Cointreau.
1/2 Cucharadita azúcar.
Hielo abundante. Muy batido y colado.

1/3 Sweet Milk.
1/3 Creme de Cacao.
1/3 Gordon Gin.
1/6 Cointreau
1/2 Teaspoonful Sugar.
Plenty of Ice.
Shake well and strain; then serve.

ROSE

1/3 Gin Gordon.
1/3 Calvados Apple Jack.
1/3 Vermouth Nolly Plat.
1/2 Cucharadita Granadina.
1 Cáscara de limón.
Hielo menudo. Batido y colado. Sírvase con guindas.

1/3 Gordon Gin.
1/3 Calvados Apple Jack.
1/3 Nolly Prat Vermouth.
1/2 Teaspoonful Grenedine.
1 Lemon Peel.
Plenty Cracked Ice.
Shake well and strain into cocktail glass.

RUM COCKTAIL

En un vaso de 10 onzas.
Hielo menudo.
Una ramita hierba buena.
La cáscara de un limón verde con el jugo exprimido dentro.
1/2 Cucharadita de azúcar.
1 Gota Angostura.
1/2 Cucharadita de Curacao.
2 Onzas Ron Bacardi.
Agítese de un vaso para el otro. Sírvase colado.

Use a 10-once glass.
Cracked Ice.
1 Sprig pepper-mint.
1 Unripe Lemon Peel,
Squeezing juice in glass.
1/2 Teaspoonful Sugar.
1 Dash Angostura.
1/2 Teaspoonful Curacao.
2 Ounces Bacardi Rum.
Shake lightly and strain; then, serve.

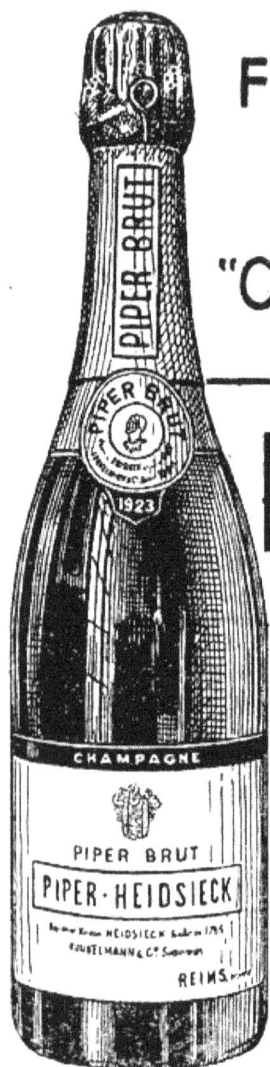

FRANCE'S GIFT
TO THE
"CONNAISSEUR"

PIPER-HEIDSIECK

ESTAB. EN 1785.

Champagne

Kunkelmann & Cie.
Reims.

RUM DAISSY

Una copa llena de hielo menudo.
1 Gota Angostura.
½ Cucharadita de Cha-
treusse amarillo.
2 Onzas Ron Bacardí.
½ Cáscara limón con jugo.
½ Cucharadita azúcar.
Unas ramitas hierba buena.
Dos guindas y frutas esta-
ción. Sírvase sin colar.

1 Glass full of cracked ice.
1 Dash Angostura.
½ Teaspoonful Yellow
Chartreuse.
2 Ounces Bacardi Rum.
½ Unsqueezed Lemon Peel.
½ Teaspoonful Sugar.
Several sprigs pepper-mint.
Two cherries and season
fruits. Stir and serve without straining.

RUBI SILVER COCKTAIL

½ Sloe Gin Gordon.
½ Cherry Brandy.
El jugo de un limón.
½ Clara de huevo.
Hielo abundante muy
batido y colado

½ Gordon Gin.
½ Cherry Brandy.
1 Lemon juice.
½ White of an eggs.
Plenty ice. Shake very
well and strain.

SEVILLANA

1 Gota Angostura.
½ Cucharadita Curacao.
½ Cucharadita azúcar.
½ Vermouth Martini Rossi.
½ Ginebra Bols.
Varias ramitas hierba buena
con su jugo.
Agítese de un vaso para
otro. Sírvase colado y con un
par de guindas.

1 Dash Angostura.
½ Teaspoonful Sugar.
½ Teaspoonful Curacao.
½ Martini Rossi Vermouth.
½ Bols Gin.
1 Lemon Peel unsqueezed.

Stir and strain; then, serve
with a couple of cherries.

SILVER FIZZ

2 Onzas Gin Gordon.	2 Ounces Gordon Gin.
1 Cucharadita azúcar.	1 Teaspoonful Sugar.
1 Clara de huevo.	The White of 1 Egg.
Jugo de ½ limón.	The Juice of ½ Lemon.
Varias gotas menta blanca.	Several Dashes of white Creme de Menthe.
Muy batido y colado.	Shake well and strain into glass.

SOBERANO BRANDY HIGHBALL

Vasito de Cognac Soberano.	Small glass of Soberano Cognac.
Pedazo de hielo.	Plenty Cracked Ice.
¼ agua mineral aparte.	¼ of mineral water.

SEVENTH HEAVEN

La piel de un limón sin jugo.	1 Lemon Peel Squeezed.
½ Cucharadita Fernet-Branca.	½ Teaspoonful Fernet-Branca.
½ Vermouth Martini Rossi	½ Martini Rossi Vermouth.
½ Sloe Gin Gordon.	½ Gordon's Sloe Gin.
¼ Cucharadita azúcar.	¼ Teaspoonful Sugar.
Hielo. Batido y colado.	Cracked Ice.
Sírvase con varias almendras o nueces.	Shake well and strain into cocktail glass. Serve with several almonds or walnuts.

JABON DE HIEL DE VACA DE CRUSELLAS

THE SECRET OF BEAUTIFUL FACES DURING A CENTURY.

RHUM QUINQUINA DE CRUSELLAS

REFRESHES AND CURES THE SCALP. PREVENTS DANDRUFF. BEAUTIFIES AND CURLS THE HAIR.

TWO PRICELESS ARTICLES OF WORDLY RENOWN.

56

SUMMER WELLES SPECIAL COCKTAIL

½ Vermouth italiano.
½ Whisky C. Club.
1 Cucharadita de Amor Picón.
½ Cucharadita de Curacao.
1 Gota de Angostura Bitters.
½ Cucharadita de azúcar.
Hielo menudo, batido y colado.
Sírvase con una ramita de hierba buena y dos guindas verdes.

½ Italian Vermouth.
½ C. Club Whisky.
1 Teaspoonful Picon Love.
½ Teaspoonful Curacao.
1 Drop Angostura Bitters.
½ Teaspoonful of sugar
Crushed ice.
Shake and strain.
Serve with Peppermint and 2 green cherries.

SUISSE

½ Abshinte Pernot.
½ Agua natural.
¼ Anisette o bien jarabe natural.
½ Clara de huevo.
Hielo menudo.
Batido y sírvase colado.

½ Pernot Absinthe.
½ Natural
Water.
½ Anisette of
Plain Syrup.
½ Egg.
Cracked Ice.
Shake well and
s t r a i n ; then
serve.

SNOW BALL

1/3 Gin Gordon.	1/3 Gordon Gin.
1/3 Parfait Amour.	1/3 Parfait Amour.
1/3 Crema Menta verde.	1/3 Green Creme de Men-the.
1/3 Leche fresca.	1/3 Fresh milk.
Hielo menudo. Muy batido y colado.	Cracked Ice. Shake well and strain into cocktail glass.

SHERRY FLIP

1 Copa Jerez Seco La Ina.	1 Glass Dry Sherry Wine.
1 Cucharadita azúcar.	1 Teaspoonful Sugar.
1 Huevo completo.	1 Egg.
Hielo abundante.	Plenty cracked ice.
Muy batido y sírvase colado y adornado con canela en polvo.	Shake well and strain into cocktail glass. Serve with powdered cinnamon on top.

SMOKED COCKTAIL

½ Cucharadita Curacao.	½ Teaspoonful Curacao.
1 Cucharadita azúcar.	1 Teaspoonful Sugar.
2 Onzas Scoth Whiskey.	2 Ounces Scotch. Whiskey.
Hierba buena.	1 Sprig Peppermint.
½ Limón con su jugo y cáscara.	½ Lemon (juice and peel).
Hielo menudo.	Cracked Ice.
Agítese de u nvaso para el otro y sírvase colado.	Shake lightly and strain; then serve.

STINGER
(After dinner drink)

½ Cognac Soberano.
½ Menta blanca.
Hielo menudo. Bien batido y colado.

½ Soberano Cognac.
½ White Creme de Menthe
Cracked ice.
Shake well and strain in cocktail glass.

SLOE GIN FIZZ

2 Onzas Sloe Gin Gordon.
½ Cucharadita Curacao.
½ Cucharadita Amer Picón.
½ Cucharadita azúcar.
Jugo de ½ limón verde.
Hielo abundante. Batido y colado.

2 Ounces Gordon's Sloe Gin
½ Teaspoonful Curacao.
½ Teaspoonful Amer Picon.
½ Teaspoonful Sugar.
The Juice of ½ Unripe Lemon Plenty of ice.
Shake well and strain in cocktail glass.

S. O. S. COCKTAIL

1/2 Cucharadita Raspail.
1/3 Vermouth Nolly Prat.
1/2 Vermouth Martini Rossi
1/3 Old Tom Gin.
Hielo menudo.
Agítese sin batirlo y sirvase colado con lascas de piña longitudinales y varias guindas.

1/2 Teaspoonful Raspail.
1/3 Nolly Prat Vermouth.
1/2 Martini Rossi Vermouth
1/3 Old Tom Gin.
Cracked Ice.
Stir and strain; then, serve with slices of pineapple and several cherries.

TEQUILA COCKTAIL

Un vaso de 20 onzas de Tequila puro.	In a 20 ounces glass put Tequila puro.
El jugo de un limón.	A lemon juice.
Una cucharadita de azúcar.	1 Teaspoonful of sugar.
Una gota de Angostura.	1 Drop Angostura.
Hielo abundante, bien batido y colado.	Plenty of ice, shake well and strain.

SAN MARTIN

1|3 Ginebra Old Tom.	1|3 Old Tom Gin.
1|3 Vermouth Noly Prat.	1|3 Nolly Prat Vermouth.
1|3 Vermouth Martini Rossi.	1|3 Martini Rossi Vermouth.
1 Cucharadita de Anisette.	1|3 Martini Rossi Vermouth.
1 Gota de Angostura.	1 Teaspoonful Anisette.
Hielo menudito.	1 Dash Angostura.
Muévase con una cuchara y cuélese. Al borde de la copa humedezcase con limón y azúcar.	Plenty of cracked ice. Stir with a spoon. Strain and serve in coktail glass. Wet brim of glass with lemon and sugar.

ORANGE BLOSSON

½ Jugo naranja.	½ Orange Juice.
½ Gin Gordon.	½ Gordon Gin.
½ Cucharada Granadina.	½ Teaspoonful Grenedine. Cracked Ice.
Hielo menudo. Batido y colado.	Shake well and strain into a cocktail glass.

"La Estrella"

BOMBONES DE LICOR
TROPICALES
y de Frutas y Jaleas
Crema de Guayaba

La Marca de Calidad

LIQUOR FILLED and TROPICAL FRUIT FLAVORED CANDIES

Obispo 88   Sn. Rafael 8

62

OJEN COCKTAIL

2 Onzas Ojén.
2 Gotas Angostura.
Hielo abundante. Batido y colado.

2 Ounces Ojen.
2 Dashes Angostura.
Plenty of Cracked ice.
Shake well and strain; then serve.

OLD SMUGGLER'S AWAKEN

2 Onzas Ginebra Bols.
1 Cucharada de azúcar.
1 Gota Angostura.
1 Huevo entero.
La piel de un limón verde.
Hielo menudo. Batido y colado.
Adórnese con canela en polvo.

2 Ounces Bols Gin.
1 Spoonful Sugar.
1 Dash Angostura.
1 Egg.
1 Lemon Peel.
Cracked Ice.
Shake well and strain into cocktail glass.
Powdered cinnamon on top.

OLD FASHION WHISKEY

En un vaso de old fashion lleno de hielo.
Varias ramitas hierba buena.
1 Cáscara entera de limón exprimiéndolo adentro.
½ Cucharadita azúcar.
½ Cucharadita Curacao.
2 Onzas Rye Whiskey.
Agítese violentamente y sírvase sin colarlo adornado con lascas de piña, naranja y guindas.

1 Old-fashioned glass full of cracked ice. Several springs of pepper-mint.
1 Complete Lemon Peel. Squeeze into glass.
½ Teaspoonful Sugar.
½ Teaspoonful Curacao.
2 Ounces Rye Whiskey.
Shake well. Do not strain. Serve in glass decorated with slices of pineapple, orange and cherry.

VERMOUTH
(American Style)

2 Onzas Martín Rossi.	2 Ounces Martín Rossi.
2 Cucharadita Amer Pi-	1 Teaspoonful Amer
cón.	P con.
½ Cucharadita Curacao.	½ Teaspoonful Curacao.
1 Gota Angostura.	1 Dash Angostura.
1 Cáscara de limón.	1 Lemon Peel.
1 Ramita hierba buena.	1 Small Sprig Pepper-
½ Cucharadita de azúcar.	mint.
Hielo menudo. Batido y	½ Teaspoonful Sugar.
colado. Sirvase con un par	Cracked ice.
de guindas.	Shake well and strain into
	cocktail glass. Serve with
	a couple of cherries.

VERMOUTH
(Colonial Style)

Un vaso old fashion lleno de hielo menudo.	1 O'd Fashioned Glass of crushed ice.
½ Cucharadita de azúcar.	½ Teaspoonful Sugar.
1 Cáscara de limón expri- mido dentro del vaso.	1 Lemon Peel Squeezed into the glass.
1 Gota de Angostura.	1 Dash Angostura.
1 Ramita hierba buena.	1 Sprig Pepper-mint.
½ Cucharadita de Curacao.	½ Teaspoonful Curacao.
1 Cucharadita Amer Picón.	1 Teaspoonful Amer Picon.
2 Onzas Vermouth Martini Rossi para llenar el vaso.	2 Ounces Martini Rossi Vermouth to fill glass.
Agítese violentamente y sír- vase con un colador ade- cuado.	Shake well and strain, then serve.

VELVET PUNCH

½ Guinness Sout Beer,
½ Champagne.
Todo frío y servido al natural.

½ Guinness Sout Beer.
½ Champagne.
Serve cold, but without cracked Ice.

VERSAILLES CLUB

½ Dubonnet.
½ Cognac Soberano.
½ Cucharadita de Curacao.
Enfríese y cuélese sin batirlo.

½ Dubonnet.
½ Soberano Cognac.
½ Teaspoonful Curacao.
Do ot shake. Drain and serve very cold.

ZAZERAC

2 Onzas Rye Whiskey,

1 Cucharadita Anisette.

2 Gotas Angostura.

La piel completa de un limón verde.

Hielo menudo. Batido y colado.

El borde de la copa impregnado de limón y azúcar.
Con la piel del limón dentro en espiral.

2 Ounces Rye Whisky.

1 Teaspoonful Anisette.

2 Dashes Angostura.

1 Lemon Peel.

Cracked Ice.

Shake well and strain. Brim of glass frosted with sugar and lemon. Lemon peel inside then glass.

PEGGY NILES
(Special)

2 Onzas Ron Bacardí Carta Oro.	2 Ounces Bacardi Rum Carta Oro.
½ Jugo de un limón.	Juice of half a lemon.
1 Cucharadita Elíxir Bacardí.	½ Teaspoonful sugar.
½ Cucharadita azúcar.	1 Teaspoonful of Elíxir Bacardí.
Batido eléctricamente con hielo frapé, sírvase en una copa de cocktail.	Shake in a electric shaker with crushed ice. Serve in a cocktail glass.

COCKTAIL GLORIA
(Delicado a Gloria de la C. M.)

3/3 Ginebra Gordon's.	3/3 Gordon's Gin.
1/3 Vino Dubonet.	2 Dashes of Ajenjo.
2 Gotas de Ajenjo.	1/3 Dubonet wine.
Enfríese con hielo abundante; sírvase en copa de cocktail.	Cool well with plenty of ice serve in a cocktail glass.

PALM OLIVE
Cocktail Especial

½ Jugo de toronja.	½ Juice of a crape fruit.
½ Ginebra Gordon's.	½ Gordon's gin.
1 Cucharadita menta verde.	½ Teaspoonful green mint.
Hielo menudo, abundante y bien batido y colado, sírvase en un vaso de 6 onzas.	Plenty of ice shake well and straim serve in a 6 ounces glass.

¿Está usted inapetente?... Es porque quiere. Recuerde esta fórmula: "DE TRES COPAS" UNA COPA, ANTES DE TOMAR LA SOPA. El coñac "Tres Copas" de González Byass, Jerez de la Frontera, está respaldado por un siglo de celosa vigilancia sobre la pureza de los vinos y coñacs de esta firma.

CORONEL BATISTA
Especial

½ Vermouth Torino.
½ Ron Carta Blanca.
   Jugo de ½ limón.
½ Cucharadita de azúcar.
Bátase perfectamente con
hielo menudo, cuélese y sírvase con una lasca de piña
y dos guindas.

½ Vermouth Torino.
½ Rum Carta Blanca.
   The juice of ½ lemon.
½ Teaspoounful of sugar.
Shake well and strain with
crushed ice serve with 1
slice of pineapple and two
cherries.

P. ARANGO
Cocktail Especial

½ Vermouth Nolly Prat.
½ Bacardi Carta Oro.
Enfriese y cuélese "no batido". Sirvase con una cáscara
de naranja, en copa alta.

½ Vermouth Nolly Prat.
½ Bacardi Carta Oro.
Cool and strain "do not
shake". Serve with a orange
peel in a cocktail glass.

PISCO PUNCH

Jugo de 1 limón.
Una gota Angostura.
½ Cucharaditas azúcar.
2 Onzas aguardiente de
Uva bien batido y colado.
Sirvase en una copa impreg-
nada de anisette con 2 guindas.

Juice of 1 lemon.
Dash Angostura.
2 Ounces crape brandy.
Cracked ice shake well and
strain serve in a glass weth
anisette and two cherries.

Hay muchos rones;

pero sólo

un **BACARDÍ**

Casa Genaro Suárez

LAS MEJORES FRUTAS DEL PAIS

Angel Suárez y Co.

Mercado de Colón No. 15, Habana, Cuba

www.ingramcontent.com/pod-product-compliance
Lightning Source LLC
Chambersburg PA
CBHW050954050426
42337CB00051B/1199